POEMS FOR JEREMY CORBYN

POEMS FOR JEREMY CORBYN

EDITED BY
MERRYN WILLIAMS

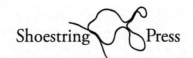
Shoestring Press

Printed by imprintdigital
Upton Pyne, Exeter
www.imprintdigital.com

Typesetting by narrator
www.narrator.me.uk
info@narrator.me.uk
033 022 300 39

Cover design by Rosalind Evans
r.evans@mail.com

Cover image by Rwendland, modified by Rosalind Evans
https://commons.wikimedia.org/wiki/File%3AJeremy_Corbyn%2C_Tolpuddle_2016%2C_2.jpg By Rwendland (Own work) [CC BY-SA 4.0 (http://creativecommons.org/licenses/by-sa/4.0)], via Wikimedia Commons from Wikimedia Commons

Published by Shoestring Press
19 Devonshire Avenue, Beeston, Nottingham, NG9 1BS
(0115) 925 1827
www.shoestringpress.co.uk

First published 2016
© Copyright: the individual authors

The moral rights of the authors have been asserted.

ISBN 978-1-910323-66-3

CONTENTS

INTRODUCTION

Summer 2016. The number of refugees is the highest since 1945. The long agony of the Middle East continues and spills over into Europe, causing multiple tragedies. Respected voices talk about 'the coming war with Russia' and suggest that mankind has only an even chance of surviving the twenty-first century. At home, we vote to disengage from our European neighbours, hate crimes shoot up and two good people are killed, apparently because of their religious/political beliefs. And always in the background there is hunger, preventable disease, the possibility of nuclear war and the growing threat to planet earth.

Doesn't it seem obvious that the world ought to be run by people of vision and integrity, who believe in universal human values and who care about the next generation? And isn't it equally obvious that this is not happening? As one retired MP once told me, most politicians only think short-term. Other kinds of people exist, but we usually know little about them. 'That things are not so ill with you and me as they might have been, is half owing to the number who lived faithfully a hidden life, and rest in unvisited tombs'.

Most of us had never heard of Jeremy Corbyn until about a year ago. He had led a quiet life of public service and hundreds of people had cause to be grateful to him, but he never expected or particularly wanted to be famous. Through an extraordinary sequence of events he was propelled into the limelight and he has attracted the extremes of love and rage. He has endured a vicious storm of abuse which would break most of us, but he is popular among poets.

'Poetry makes nothing happen', it's been famously said, and poets are, on the whole, an anarchic and idiosyncratic lot. But creative people often have a clearer and longer vision than the men and women of power. In the very short time it took to organise this anthology I received dozens of contributions, and am only sorry that so many had to be left out. The fifty here included are not hymns of praise to an individual but poems written in the spirit of Jeremy Corbyn. The subjects are war and peace, human rights, the misery of excluded people in an age of

1

austerity, bullying and Brexit. Green issues too; we're invited to think about scarlet macaws, Muntjac deer, disappearing species and spiders. Those which focus on the man himself take a sceptical look at that word 'leadership'. What we need, they suggest, is not a Fuehrer-figure who tells us what to think – we've seen where that leads – 'but someone who has found a way to voice/a fractured country's need for choice/to say we'll make another kind of noise' (Nicholas Murray, 'J.C.'). There are some brilliant and extraordinary poems between these covers. I hope that you, and he, will like them.

Merryn Williams

MAIDEN SPEECH

*The people to whom I am sending you are obstinate and stubborn. Whether
they listen or fail to listen – for they are a rebellious house – they will know
that a prophet has been among them.*
– Ezekiel 2: 4–5

The new MP (where is he from again?) has swallowed more
than any other member of this house can chew.
Which he'll regurgitate until they're edgy on their padded seats
and wriggle to distract themselves and distance what he says
from how it's said.

They may admit his knack with rhetoric, but mock
his ignorance of how the world must work. He'll have no truck
with what he calls the politics of scorpions
and economics founded on a currency of thorns.

Opponents from all sides respond in speech that won't obscure
his questions though they try. They blame his ambiguity.
Each side can understand the other. One side pretends they can't.

This frowning man lets bitter words slide smoothly from his tongue
into their ears – to sabotage their balance, make them gag
and squirm like scorpions who'll sting themselves to death.

Michael Bartholomew-Biggs

REFUGEE

She came with a name
A few things, a line of English
And searching eyes,
And nothing.

Fourteen, just, big big Africa girl,
She happened in school
And never talked of war,
The massacre,

Parents cut up and lost,
Would anyone want to know
In classrooms of taunts
And segregation

Based on size and body smells
And designer labels? Hardly.
And then the day before Christmas
Her foster family evicts her.

They come over 'ere y' know
And get everything.

Neil Beardmore

4

THE SEVEN AGES OF A LABOUR M.P.

                                    At first the student,
Posing and strutting in the NUS.
Then the droning speaker, with his briefcase
And shining Sunday suit, creeping to his
Selection Committee. And then the loyalist,
Lying like trooper, with a woeful tirade
Made to his Leader's buttocks. Then an MP,
Full of strange terms, reading from autocue,
Lacking all honour, shallow and slick in quarrel,
Seeking the bubble reputation,
Ever in the camera's eye. And then the minister,
In fair round belly with free dinners lined,
Eyes insincere and clothes of formal cut,
Full of cheap lies and dodgy evasions;
And so he makes his pile. The sixth age shifts
Into the mean and cliché'd veteran,
With spectacles on nose and perks on side;
His youthful hopes, long lost, are far too wide
For his shrunk mind; and his big manly voice,
Turning again toward childish platitudes,
Repeats the old slogans. Last scene of all,
That ends this uneventful history,
Is Second Chamber, full of mere oblivion,
Sans teeth, *sans* brain, *sans* guts, *sans* principles.

                                              Ian Birchall

HOW LOW CAN THEY BOW?

Respect for war dead is not proved
By the depth of bow you're showing,
But by the mountains you have moved
To stop their numbers growing.

Janine Booth

A SCREAM IN 1890

A scream in the room that goes on for ever, long
Tidy table after table into the distance, my grandmother
Pedals harder suddenly, and stops.
Any time you stopped, you looked at the clock, and wondered
Can I rest for a moment and still catch up with the work?
This is five-and-twenty to nine, she remembers
Fifty-two years on.
                              The scream has come
From a girl a long way behind her, a needle
Has gone through somebody's thumb several tables back.
– First, a second so quiet that you could have heard a –

Then other screams, like late echoes. The girl looks at
The thumb pinned down as if it wasn't hers.
Girls from elsewhere crowd round her, they always
Said it would happen, most girls knew someone who'd done it.
It was when you were tired – but then you were always tired.
Why should careful Flora have done it?
                                          The overseer
(She thinks it was the word) shoves them all aside –
'Get back to work. No talking!' And takes a look
At the girl, at the thumb, at the blood
Spreading under the nail in the nineteenth-century sunlight.

Obediently no one talks, but they seize
Sidelong glances at each other and sit still.
They can hear his words in the silence before resuming,
Their eyes all going back to their own thumbs.
They can hear what he says, and will always remember the tone
Mr Podmore the overseer uses, applying
The discipline of his own overseers, telling Flora:
Move the wheel   *listen* to me   move it *yourself*
Move it very slowly   slowly   as slowly
As you can   that's it   that's it   Are you all right?

Alan Brownjohn

SONG OF THE KNIVES-IN-THE-BACKBENCHERS

(search "Gee, Officer Krupke" on YouTube)

Dear saintly Jezza Corbyn,
you gotta understand
that parliaments of fawning
have left us very bland.
Our voters all drive Volvos;
our agents do the same –
Golly Moses, naturally we're tame!

Gee, Jeremy Corbyn, we're sorry to say
that compromise and stalling have led us astray.
But we ain't no class traitors,
whatever you think.
Deep down inside us we're quite pink!
We are pink!

We are pink, we are pink,
we're extremely pink!
Deep inside, some parts of us are pink!

SNOWBOY: *(spoken)* That's a feel-good pinkalicious story.

ACTION: *(spoken)* Lemme tell it to the woild!

SNOWBOY: Just tell it to the Baron.

ACTION: *(sings)*
Dear kindly Baron Sparkbrook,
those lefties debate
every line in the rulebook,
but our selections were straight.
So, no one wants to choose us
but somehow we get chose?
Dodgy dossiers! Tell that to the crows!

8

DIESEL: *(as Baron)* That's it! It's just a *local*,
conshtituenshional matter!

Oh Hattersley, brother, you're such an old square;
he don't need reselecting, just a style-guru's care!
It's all that posh suiting that needs to vamoose;
he's sartorialogically confused!

ACTION I'm confused!

JETS We're confused, we're confused,
we're the most confused,
we're sartorialistically confused!

DIESEL: *(spoken, as Baron)* In the opinion of the Potty
Chamber, this stooge is confused on account
his underwear ain't speaking to his overwear.

ACTION: *(spoken)* Hey, I'm distressed on account I'm
mis-dressed!

DIESEL: So find him a wardrobe consultant – what
about IKEA?

ACTION: *(sings)*
My father wears Curvissa,
my mother is a Goth,
my nephew's all in Lycra,
my wife won't take 'em off.
My brother wears silk gaiters,
my sister wears a dress!
Goodness gracious, that's why I'm a mess!

A-RAB: *(as fashionista)* No!

Jeremy Corbyn, you're up the wrong tree;
this sap don't need a tailor but a pamphlet or three.
The Party just left him to twiddle his thumbs,
so that ideologically he's dumb!

ACTION: I am dumb!

ALL: We are dumb, we are dumb;
             we are dumb, dumb, dumb.
             Like we're ideolistically dumb!

A-RAB: In my opinion, this chump don't need no new
             threads. Political illiteritis is purely a
             educational deficit!

ACTION: Hey, I'm educationally defective!

A-RAB: So take him to an evening class! (If you can
             find one.)

ACTION: *(sings)*
             Dear kind all-knowing teacher,
             they say I need to learn
             that bosses are just leeches
             and the workers need a turn.
             It's not I'm anti-justice;
             I'm only anti-change.
             Hooray Rita! *That's* why I'm deranged!

BABY JOHN: *(as teacher)* No!
             Jeremy Corbyn, you're not making sense.
             This berk don't need a book; he needs a kick
             in the pants.
             It ain't just a question of underinformed;
             in every fibre of his being he conforms!

ACTION: I conform!

ALL: We conform, we conform!
             We just love to conform;
             point us any which way – we'll conform!

DIESEL: *(as Baron)* The trouble is he's timid.

10

A-RAB:	*(as fashionista)* The trouble is he's square.
BABY JOHN:	*(as teacher)* The trouble is he's stupid.
DIESEL:	The trouble is – he's Theirs!
A-RAB:	*(rocking gesture)* The trouble is he's floating.
BABY JOHN:	*(changes rosette to MRLP)* The trouble is he's flown!
ALL:	Corbyn, we got troubles of our own!

Gee, Jeremy Corbyn –
we're all gonna lose,
'cos no one wants a MP with yesterday's views.
Gee, Jeremy Corbyn,
what are we to do?
Gee, Jeremy Corbyn,
CURB YOU!!

Rip Bulkeley

MUNTJAC DEER AT FREELAND

The despairing voice cries
'kill the lot', as we hush
to watch a Muntjac step lightly
onto the lawn, its curved back
a delicate question mark.
        'They gorge
themselves', the tart voice persists
as we're held by the sight
of this miracle of calm,
so close, so close.

(Of evolutionary interest
for their chromosome count,
descendants of escapes
from Woburn Abbey circa 1925,
these ancient orientals
have joined our herd and increased –
two have actually been seen near Belfast,
obviously with human help).

'But so many make road-kill',
I demur, as the dainty deer
muzzles short clover and grass.
'Good', comes the vengeful reply,
'they eat all my plants!'
        'Where
do they belong, who cares',
I wonder aloud, watching
tiny migrant hooves barely dent
the damp ground.

Olivia Byard

THE SOCIALIST

He's clutching his anti-apartheid banner.
Police grip his arms,
haul him from the demo.

He's fighting for miners,
never forgets they've been
abandoned to their fate.

He's at the march in 2003
protesting against Blair's war
but millions of voices go unheard.

He's there for the junior doctors,
the steel workers, the homeless –
invisible to this Tory government.

He's being bullied by his fellow MPs,
despite reaching out to them,
including them in his shadow cabinet.

And who has his back?
We do!

Di Coffey

HOUSING CRISIS

In search of a home she trawls the council list
alert for open spaces, well-fenced – her inverse:

all self-sufficient, without mental health;
somewhere un-English where to lose herself.

Meanwhile the mind un-housed cannot create:
self's seedling cells simply self-duplicate

themselves within selves that are sunk in self-consciousness
until growing ever closer, they grow the less.

The biro starts to fade.
X marks the cross of her ethnicity.

Is there another country she can't see?
More than this black-and-white to you and me?

Deborah Cox

CANVASSING IN A SAFE TORY SEAT

We readjust our faces on the long walk
between front doors. At least it's pleasant weather
and the gardens look pretty; some of their owners
seem nice people could they see beyond these lawns.

Someone is listening to Wagner. We can hear
the dragon's snores and Wotan's patience,
and consider the wisdom of interruption.
Massive hardwood seems to sneer on us

and the knocker to smell our nervousness.
'Erwache, Wurm!' We are answered
by good breeding mouthing a smile at us,
politely blind. *'What I have, I hold. Let me sleep'*.

Would even constant water affect these stones?
What arguments can touch honest selfishness?
We trudge back, down the sweep of the drive,
and approach another Fafner's cave.

The quotations are from Wagner's Ring cycle; the one in German means
'Wake up, dragon'. Wotan is the leader of the gods, Fafner is the dragon.

Barbara Cumbers

IN THE SCILLIES

Blue sprays of agapanthus in a vase
Remember you: *Lord Wilson of Rievaulx.*
Hard to believe, as I take in your name,
Your premiership was forty years ago.
You lie in Scilly Island peace,
Above St Mary's rock-strewn Old Town Bay,
World leader, once – in headlines, on the box –
Familiar as de Gaulle or LBJ.

Pied wagtails scavenge seaweed on white sand,
A black lab chases after lobbed-up sticks;
Coming across your headstone here by chance
Suddenly takes me back to 'sixty-six,
The time of Labour's narrow win.
That spring, I'd trudged the streets of Colchester,
All kinds of hopes for progress in my head,
And canvassed for you, student volunteer.

You'd taken part in Attlee's government,
Nye Bevan's ally, aid to Beveridge,
Whose great post-war reforms (think NHS)
Marked milestones out that still defined the age.
Articulate and down-to-earth,
You'd galvanise the country from its past;
Standing for change from Tory-led misrule,
You'd build a meritocracy at last.

Economic planning, education,
I would have seen a continuity
With what I'd read of the Enlightenment
Which formed the framework of my PhD.
We welcomed Labour's new reforms,
Its liberal legislation's common sense;
Gay rights, divorce, an end to censorship;
We'd have no truck with class-bound deference.

It's forty years ago. It's history (think,
My fellow canvassers now pensioners!)
What does one make of what you made of things
In these post-Thatcher and post-modern years?
Your left v. right manoeuvrings
On Europe and on staying nuclear;
Vietnam and Biafra; UDI
Declared by Ian Smith's Rhodesia.

Financial problems plagued you; wage demands
And constant pressure from the TUC;
With runs on sterling getting worse and worse
And trade deficit grim as grim could be,
Devaluation came; no choice;
Then opposition to *In Place of Strife*
Proved something even you could not finesse,
While endless politicking defined the life

That being a Prime Minister entailed;
A daily bruising leadership hard grind;
It's not the scheming, trimming pragmatist
But non-stop stress and strain that strikes the mind;
In three months, once, ten cabinets,
And twenty ministerial speeches, too,
Two dozen cabinet committees chaired –
A 'hectic incoherence'? Muddling through?

One thinks of Brezhnev's Warsaw Pact response
To Dubcek's 1968 Prague Spring;
The march on Washington for Civil Rights,
The gunning down of Martin Luther King,
As if to mock us all, 'Get real!'
We'd had high hopes, things Burns had stood up for,
A man's a man, the worth of brotherhood;
But Birmingham pub bomb? The Six Day War?

The rip-tide of events, *realpolitik;*
It meant you were compelled to temporise
On public service ethic old ideals
And deal in grimy coin of compromise….
I watch the black lab chasing sticks,
The wagtails pecking seaweed by the bay;
Tempus imperator rerum, I read,
A sentiment straight out of Thomas Gray.

The headstone words and agapanthus blooms
Seem well set up for elegiac tropes;
What does one make of what you made of things,
Who once personified our 'sixties hopes?
A much too cautious liberal?
Or super-devious, since insecure?
Many attest your unpretentiousness,
Say how considerate and kind you were.

I guiltily contrive my version of
A 'doubts, distractions, fears' scenario,
The student canvasser an OAP,
Whose sixty-six lies four decades ago.
The couple with the dog move off.
They're young. They might believe in Cameron.
And there's a thought. What hopes, Enlightenment,
The banks near bust, recession coming on?

Simon Curtis

'Hectic incoherence' is a phrase from Philip Zeigler's biography of
Harold Wilson.

A HISTORY OF THE WORLD IN 101 OBJECTS

And this, from the later Twentieth Century,
nineteen forty seven, to be precise,
though much in evidence to the present day.

There is a rightness about the implement,
fitting as it does the grip of both young and old,
serviceable under all conditions of politics and duress
and in all climates, extremes of hot and cold.

The quality of manufacture ensures
a uniform and reliable performance.
Simplicity of function means it is
easily maintained in field conditions,

and, allowing for the weight, even
a child or malnourished adult may carry
and use the piece to great effect,
girl or boy, woman or man.

The arc of fire is generous,
though accuracy it may be noted
must be sacrificed to the efficacy of the scythe.

This is the Ram's Horn, the Cuerno de Chivo –
it has decorated the flags of causes and nations
from Moscow to Mozambique to Mexico.
It has been converted into a guitar.

It is said that the inventor of the piece
had ambitions to be a poet:
instead, wounded in the defence
of his homeland, he designed this.

And for over sixty years who is to say
more or fewer poems have come from its use:
the chattering metre, the rhyme,
the stanzas and epics of the AK?

Tony Curtis

THE BIGGER PICTURE

9th April 2003

You saw it on TV – the footage showed
the mighty Ozymandian overthrow,
the falling statue and the cheering crowd –
and probably believed that it was so.
But see the picture taken from above
in black and white, a single grainy still
which irresistibly reminds one of
the early work of Cecil B DeMille.
The close-up cheering of a small élite
was caught on careful cameras, but not
the roadblocks at the end of every street
lest uninvited extras spoiled the shot
of History being created there
in one small corner of an empty square.

Ann Drysdale

ONE MORE STEP TOWARD OBLIVION

I walk the same path into the city
graffiti flaked on broken cemented hips
houses lathered in bind weed and ivy,
where the moon patrols the earth's circling lips.
On this day an island lost its soul,
the lion sipped milk from the carcass of Europe
Austerity Kings control the beating veins
that stir and corrupt mouths full of shadows and no light,
I walked the same path on that day;
seeing the city in quite a different shade,
hope of a nation lay in only one man's fight.

Matthew Duggan

ANTIQUE LAND

St Quentin's castle was never completed.
There never was a battle to attack
and defend it, arrows and siege engines,
no boiling oil. The keep is little more, now,
than a pile of stone. On the road side the Gatehouse
looks like a Gatehouse, a pointed stone arch
between two towers crumbling at the edges.
Did they go on building it so massive
out of habit even when they thought they knew
that war was over for ever in these parts,
and the castle would be just a residence?
There's a civil war battlefield near here –
Stalling Down, where people walk dogs and fly kites,
with the buzz of unseen traffic in their ears.
I prefer this hill, further from the road,
where no fighters killed or maimed each other.
The symbol of oppression is a ruin
as picturesque as some Gothic folly,
which in its own way, like the broken statue
of Ramses the Second in the desert sands,
makes you more optimistic about life.

John Freeman

PRESSURE

There is no pressure on me, none whatsoever, the real pressure is when you don't have enough money to feed your kids, when you don't have a roof over your head, when you're wondering how you're going to survive. That is the real pressure in our society. Those people struggling on low pay, on zero hour contracts, that's the brutal pressure put on people every day of the week.
– Jeremy Corbyn, Durham Miners' Gala, 9th July 2016.

Headlines are a rack
the media would stretch him on,
op-ed pieces the pincers
crimped over finger or toe.

This is not pressure.

Secret ballots, back room allegiances,
resignation speeches
like bedroom doors slamming.
Slung mud and false flags flying.

This is not pressure.

Leadership contenders lurch
from the laugh-out-loud fall-out
of an am-dram coup, grasping
like zombies with a PR budget.

This is not pressure.

Pressure is no money
and children crying for food.

Pressure is homelessness,
the future invalidated
like a cancelled cheque.

Pressure is zero hours,
the leather glove tightening
on the already depleted,
the shiny briefcase snapping shut
on every last drop that was wrung.

Pressure is the brutality
applied to the vulnerable
every day of the week.

Neil Fulwood

THE LONG REACH OUT OF WAR

They will keep restoring the glass
in broken cathedrals

to carry the eye and the colours
that were shattered

They will keep restoring the stone
in bombed cathedrals

to carry the face and the idea
that were crushed

They will keep carrying the burden
of destroyed cathedrals

even as the ashes blow back

Humanity
keeping faith with itself
even as the ashes blow back

Katherine Gallagher

THE WORK ETHIC

Democracy is vulnerable to viruses,
health problems, cancers;
to having its legs blown away,
its tongue severed.

It can be seen on crutches at demonstrations,
on Zimmer frames in workplaces.

It never applies for a sick-note
or a chance to doss on a beach.

When depressed it thinks of its childhood
in Greek states,
teenage years in communes.

You'd think it would seek a pension
but it wakes daily to a bowl of porridge,
goes off to work whistling.

Owen Gallagher

HAVE WITH YOU TO SAVILE ROW, or A PLEASANT SATIRE OF A SON'S WARDROBE PACKED WITH HIS MOTHER'S WISDOM, NEWLY BROUGHT UP OUT OF WITNEY IN OXFORDSHIRE AND DESPATCHED ON WEDNESDAY LAST TO THE MEMBER FOR ISLINGTON NORTH

Clothes make the man
that's what my mother says,
and it's known for a truth
throughout the civilised world.
So in that scruffy jacket
can we be the same species?
In those baggy, creased trousers
can you be truly human?
                          Put on a proper suit.

You can trust a man with a tie
that's what my mother says
and it's known for a truth
throughout the civilised world.
So what do you call that
piece of cloth round your collar?
Are you Slipknot or Windsor?
Tell-Truth or Tell-a-Lie?
                          Do up your tie.

Words are the dress of thought
that's what my mother says
and it's known for a truth
throughout the civilised world.
So what are you thinking of,
keeping Mum when the band
strikes up our six patriot notes?
Fill your lungs full of air,
                          sing the national anthem.

When the argument's lost,
get the man, say the orators,
and no one recalls, for now,
how you shafted my argument.
So when the progressives come
in beards, trainers and torn jeans
I'll straighten my tie, shoot a cuff,
and, quoting my mother, tell them
                    No need to get personal.

John Gohorry

RED

Red fades in the sunlight
they say, like a pigment
from the spine of my books
in a south facing room.

Yet here a spirit endures
in the glare away from shadows,
though pursued
by a world of etiolated beige.

No peace in your search for peace
or attempt to forge a hoe
from Britannia's trident prongs,
but still the scarlet hue is left

so long as hope remains
and the light doesn't fade.

Adrian Green

TORY STORY

When she jumped in front of the train
she wasn't thinking of the open-mouthed woman
on the jostling platform
who would hear the thud as she lay awake
at 3 am for years.

She didn't consider the driver whose second
jumper this was in a week
who couldn't break out of believing
it was all his fault.

She didn't think of the passengers late
for work, missing appointments,
cursing this person who ruined their day.

She didn't think of the benefits officer
guilty at what he'd done to fill
his weekly sanctions quota.

All she could see was the month ahead.
Empty fridge, rent arrears, the beckoning street.

Nicki Griffin

WHAT YOU TOOK HOME WITH YOU FROM THE NIGHT SHIFT

That stuff so percussive
and monotonous about how
you look, your availability,
that you know so well
you could mouth along with it;
that stony look you summon up
which leaves you wanting
in so many ways
that lurk beneath the pillow
through fragmented days.

The non-standard shapes
and sizes on the night bus.
The tarnished gleam
of the generous: the handle
of an entrance
that you might have polished
given half the chance.

Echoing banter
that doesn't concern you
from the white tiles
your sponge travels
ad nauseam, a wet desert
that begins to talk back to you
from the ceramic solitude.

Third job of the night,
the similar faces,
The hum.

The way they pay five
pounds an hour
for you to pay your way:
the indifference
of the hand with the small cash.

The extent of your corruption:
a Danish pastry in your pocket
as tired as you are.

The Caribbean yacht
that carried you away
on your break at two-thirty
that trailed tropical fish
for the rest of the night.
The aching hip at three.

Steve Griffiths

AT THE MARQUIS OF GRANBY

'You're the most popular "unpopular man"
I've ever met'. He seemed to like that
yet his watchful, restrained, unruffled expression
didn't change much. Second-rate sound bite
and slightly strained wit were what I would
be brightly delivering. We'd hardly converse.

Easy-going, though with a rhinoceros hide,
he was what I expected. I was worse
than my best throughout: stupidly cheery
as if trying to coerce the man into liking me.
His eyes said 'Relax' but not 'Be merry'.
Did he do Christmas, or was it all 'steely

sense of purpose'? The beer we both drank
did not soften my edginess. He politely asked,
'Which part of Wales?' I answered (I think
a mite defensively, a hillbilly tasked
with explaining why there was straw in his hair).
'I like the country', he said, 'but don't get

out often enough to quiet skies, clean air.
When you're in Westminster you can forget
you ever yomped over the Cotswolds'. I smiled.
The Cotswolds – that toffee-nosed enclave where
most things are manicured, few are wild,
and a new Range Rover will always appear

from nowhere. It was hard to know what to say.
I kept off politics: too big a field
for our Saturday chat. 'So, Jeremy,
do you have downtime – or is it all shield
and sword and a matter of watching your back?'
'I get by fine', he said, 'just fine.

After thirty-three years tied up in the sack
of the Commons, you learn to respond with sublime
indifference to fools. There are plenty of them.
Steer a straight course, whatever the weather'.
He looked at his watch. I guessed it was 'Time
gentlemen please'. 'I won't have another',

he said, and got up. I rose, too, and shook
his hand, and the worth of what we had said
left a spell it would take an aeon to break,
a glimpse of the future, a new fountainhead.

Paul Groves

THE ANTHROPOCENE

Everything's mobile in this time of global flows:
money, people, goods, bacteria and disease.
Something's affecting frogs, bats, bees and now the trees –
too set in their ways for new climates and viruses.
>   *How were we to know?*

A fungus gnaws away at bats in hibernation
in New England: 'White-nose'. The bats wake up and fly
in search of prey in mid-winter. Six million die.
A European fungus – a probable extinction.
>   *We were not to know.*

Have all the Golden Frogs now gone from Panama?
When an African fungus smears spores on their skin
it closes down their osmo-regulation system.
Watch them wave goodbye to Sir David and his camera.
>   *How were we to know?*

Great Auks were favoured by the early mariners,
easy to catch as picking fruit and good to eat.
Birds were used for fuel, their fellows fried with the heat –
the last Great Auks were killed in Iceland for collectors.
>   *We were not to know.*

We're still working our way through the planetary menu,
just finishing the 'charismatic' megafauna –
why take an aspirin when there's White Horn Rhino powder?
Just one last slice of Bluefin Tuna – then adieu.
>   *How were we to know?*

We are as Gods so, of course, we're having a blast:
the first species to enact, wilfully or not –
and as effectively as some vast meteorite –
a mass extinction. It's the sixth. Our first and last.
>   *We were not to know.*

Nearing the climax of the climate wars, our slow
commanders somehow can't provide decisive orders –
the attrition goes on with chainsaws and Toyotas.
There's a soughing in the trees: *You were not to know?*
  How could you not know?

                                        Mark Haworth-Booth

With acknowledgments to Elizabeth Kolbert's *The Sixth Extinction*
(2014) and Wilfred Owen's 'Exposure'.

IN THE JOHN RYLANDS LIBRARY, MANCHESTER

'A fair day's wages for a fair day's work'
was what they asked, the Ancoats Brotherhood.
You hear their voices still, half choked with soot
and drifting heavenward like the city's smoke
while in the library the altered air
of knowledge filters round the hide-bound texts.
Philanthropy in this world. For the next,
printed indulgences, bibles, culture
in all its variants. Is Rylands' coin
enough to buy his place among the saints?
He paid the going rate: they've no complaints.
A devil coughs and coughs and coughs again.
A fair day's hire. Define it if you can.
'Half what you'd have to pay a gentleman'.

Stuart Henson

ON YOUR UNSUITABILITY FOR HIGH OFFICE

you loved me as a loser, but now you're worried that I just might win
– Leonard Cohen

for J.C.

The minute they realise
you might succeed in changing
more than the occasional
light bulb in the new
old community centre,
where the anti-apartheid
meetings used to happen;

the late Lord Lambton
climbs out from between
two prostitutes and into
the next available issue
of the *Daily Express*
to urge votes for anyone
but you; Earl Haig

gets up from his grave
to bang the table and tell us
you've not successfully
organised enough death
to properly understand
Britain's defence needs
in the twenty-first century.

The *Telegraph* mutters
into its whiskers about your lack
of experience – how you never once
so much as successfully destroyed a bank;
as former comedians gather

in darkest Norwich and Lincolnshire
to speak of your beige zip-up jackets.

LBC Radio exclusively reveals your plan
to give each failed asylum seeker,
and anyone who's ever
taken an axe to a child,
their own seat in
the House of Lords;
the same day, *The Spectator*
gives retired General
Franco space to expose your
long term associations
with known vegetarians
and Mexican importers
of fair trade coffee.

While on Radio Four's *Women's Hour*
the former editor of the *News of The World*
and Dame Myra Hindley agree:
the last thing this country needs
right now is you.

Kevin Higgins

SONNET 94

Some are broken, broken people, broken horses;
they have the sag in the shoulders, the defeated air.
I've seen them in respite care, in rescue homes,
curled up or nearly staggering, just about upright;
for the onlooker there's such sadness there,
such compassion for fellow creatures who have buckled at last.
I think of Nietzsche cradling the whipped horse
which broke the floodgates of his own black tide.
Believe me, I've been there, crashed and burned,
left to rise or fall by some who would 'break me as a man',
the unjust war of all against one, colleagues red in tooth and claw;
and I stooped and stumbled and limped a few yards at a time,
and there are days when I still see the taut lips of the enemy
and there are days when I can't fight the *normal* ones who
know they're right.

Norton Hodges

SI VIS PACEM, PARA BELLUM

Promote virginity through fornication.
Guarantee chastity by being a whore.
Stockpile your weapons, bring peace to the nation.
'If you want peace, you must prepare for war'.

Stephen Horsfall

THE TREE COUNCIL

(Tolpuddle, 1832)

Under the sycamore's shade
our secret council gathered,
whispers joining the breeze.

We knew gentle blades would fly
just as others spread and grew
in the many places of the desperate.

The canopy enough to hide
our vows and our union,
our shares of the plough.

Six of us sat with promises,
knowing that to bend
was not to break in storms;

knowing that the masters
were experts with their axes ;
how easily resolve could be splintered.

There was a future, but no fruit
that we could reach and pick
to feed our needy families.

I spoke up, my brothers agreed,
each plan was a wind
to carry and plant those seeds.

Mike Jenkins

TELL ME LIES ABOUT THE AUSTERITY PLAN

In homage to the inimitable Adrian Mitchell, and, of course, JC.

So we've been run down by the 'truth' again.
The recovery will be where and when?
And if we need a wheelchair –
no chance! Austerity's the plan.

Saw the Blairites walk away.
It's not for us, the people, but what the MPs say.
And so the pound's gone down the pan;
put NHS in Hunt's steely hand,
and the plotters deny that JC's the man.

Close your eyes, what future do you see?
The expenses are blown by dodgy MPs.
So blind our eyes with Brexit,
pay Boris for his blunders,
Job-Seeker those in wheelchairs,
tell us lies about the Trade Deal plans.

I can smell the rats from over here. Use your brains;
they've sabotaged thinking, flushed education down the drain.
So fill our minds with soundbites,
jab out our eyes with UKIP,
blame the Poles for Hitler,
and the media's a Tory brand.

Where were you at the time of the crime?
In the Members' bar with a flask of wine.
So chain our tongues with anthems,
fill our minds with Lotto
and the Arms Trade's vats with silver,
steal the benefits and wheelchairs.
Let Xenophobia out of the can.

Well you put your ballot paper in;
you take new membership right out;
you take an honest leader, and try to shake him all about .
No need for an election
or the referendum vows,
just tape any mouths that protest,
blind us to social injustice,
sell Human Rights for pottage,
slander an honest leader,
and tell lies to discredit Corbyn's plan.

Helen Kidd

CASTLE CORBENIC

What moves inside this castle, Peredur?[1]
Is it the bleeding king,
reflected as an infinite regression
of black boys bleeding, white boys bleeding,
bleeding and fishing, just like all boys do?

Why does the spear drop blood,
pooling over the cracks and sinking in?
(Don't tread there, said their mothers. But they were boys.)

***

We can't afford it,
money for 'the arts', what,
pay a bird to sing? a fool to gabble?
That never led to anything but trouble;
just look at how they go round stirring it,
more castle money makes them nearly ungovernable.

We can't afford to let them loose, of course not.
Without the power to terrify our peers
we're nothing, targets for obliteration.
No, I repeat, we can't. We can't afford
to squander on the poor what can be used
for something worthwhile, like to feed our growth.

Look! What can they give back?
In real, proportionate terms, say, what?
By definition they don't offer much!
They can eat biscuits from the Sally Army.

---

[1] Peredur, in Celtic myth, was Perceval, who entered the Grail Castle,
but missed the opportunity to heal the wounded Fisher King and
fulfil the destiny of the Grail when he did not ask the questions in his
heart. Corbenic was the name of the castle in later versions in which
Galahad, son of Elaine of Corbenic, was the knight in the hot spot.

What is so bright inside? What's in the dish,
carried along unending corridors
by a girl hardly bigger than the dish,
dress sown with daisies. Is it something live?
                              Why don't you ask,
you, standing on the black door's other side?
Ask! There's the old promenade, the limping king,
the corridors of boys, lost sovereignty.
Is there a god inside?

***

We can't afford
to let go of the means of terrifying,
putting the frighteners on those who might
try better, kill us all or terrify us;
we can't afford it; can't possibly stop
contaminating air and earth, sea, rivers,
even the whirling spaces between stars
with goods we made express to kill or maim
(now menacing just every child conceived
for twice two hundred years). What, us? pay now?
Cash for the soil we live upon –
us, shell out for this great big lump of food,
this shelter, this old anchor – you say what?
we should dispense real paper to protect it?

***

Oh, Peredur, the platter! Say it! now!
dump the advice your elders gave, just speak!
But it's too late.
Galahad, he was decorative, but still
a man with a clean heart, who'd speak the truth
whatever the occasion or the context.
The castle still persists, the king still lame.

47

Truth is a river, moving ever in,
for each who has a tongue it's in one place.
And that's the place, past grandeur and past cowardice
past what might pass as courage looking on,
that must be reached today.
One tongue will speak it, and the undammed flow
of consequences roar out from the stone
of the deep bed set in this island's green.

Louise Larchbourne

THE BLAME

My eighth birthday. 'But please, don't invite *him*!'
I knew which friend was meant, the one I'd scour
lane and hedgerow with, break open conkers'
shoe-tan gloss, or haul down hips and haws
his whiskery gran would steep, then store for wine.

Was that the problem? Her wet-eyed cackle,
'that'll put lead in your pencil', as each filled glass
was plonked in front of visitors. Or his mother,
seams painted up her legs. 'She's taught him words
no decent boy should know, let alone use'.

'I've got ter go in when mi bleddy mam's bin lav',
he yelled over the fence once, to cancel
our morning's plan. Common, that was it. So,
a dull, sulky party, and who to blame?
Years later I had the answer. Bloody England.

Bloody class. The common bloody shame.

John Lucas

THE CHALK FAIRY

We must all fight for a society that is more decent, secure and fair, and where
no one facing homelessness is cast aside
– J.C., 22nd December 2015.

Each night I traipse
the streets of London,
drawing chalk lines
round homeless people
sleeping rough.

I've found
that, even in the early hours
of Christmas Day,
there's no shortage of bodies
to draw my outlines round:
London's one big crime scene
every single day of the year.

Thomas McColl

GENTLE GIANTS

Some women are attracted
to alpha males, who rant
and rave, control the universe,
behave as though they were
the only ones who mattered.

I prefer the gentle men,
giants who can dance
on light feet, carry babies
in their arms, listen
to the conversation
of those whose voices are
much softer than their own.

Alwyn Marriage

J.C.

Like sheep who've scattered to the field's high corner,
the commentariat – now hunted fauna –
together cling.
The practised put-downs, and the usual sneers,
predictable pandering to baser fears,
the lazy tricks that served for years
no longer sing.

Pundits and pollsters, penny-a-liners,
effortless liars and maligners,
pieces pitched,
to *Guardian* or 4 no longer hack it.
The *zeitgeist*'s moved; they can no longer track it
and there's a note inside the salary packet:
you're ditched!

Chancellor Osborne's undeterred,
and gives his underlings the word:
attack!
Class-warrior of an antique kind
he makes his colleagues of one mind
to hound the workers from behind.
A pack

of snapping Tory dogs
emerging from the autumn fogs
exult.
The 'enemy within' attracts their curses
(that's dinner ladies, carers, nurses
who learn there's little in their purses).
It's the cult

of settling scores, unleashing dogs of war
(though strikes are fewer than before).
They winch
their arses to the saddle, salivating,

excited by the prey that's waiting,
eased by commentators' Left-baiting:
a cinch.

Their anti-union bill's revealed,
and like a rotten fruit when peeled
it's vile
inside: more harsh than any iron regime
has yet to implement, or even dream,
where strikers must declare the theme
of any Tweet

before releasing it or face a fine or gaol:
that's Britain now where oppositions fail
to fight.
Until J.C. discovers that the old and young
are eager to bite back, give tongue
to protest, scrap the song that's sung
stage Right.

Its mandate twenty-five per cent of votes,
the Government each day emotes:
'Reform!'
until our ears become resistant to the sound,
detect the lie that is its constant ground,
refuse the claim that they have found
a 'norm'.

Corbyn's no knight in shining vest,
or bright Messiah from the West
(he'd say)
but someone who has found a way to voice
a fractured country's need for choice,
to say we'll make another kind of noise:
No way!

Nicholas Murray

THE FERRYMAN

I often think of that unnamed road in Nagasaki
where the zero of her breast remained untouched by fire
as her daughter suckled to live through Fat Man's crucible.

I often think of the man who found them as Pompeii ornaments
standing there knowing he would soon pay Charon at the shore,
as he drifted away from *Sake* and a sword born of fire and water.

I often think of Nagasaki mothers as sheets for their babies.
We are going to sleep in a manger of weird flames,
death will display us like screaming white logs.

I often think of those things the bomb breathed upwards –
tatami mats and door knobs found high in mountains,
dentures welded to the bones of a charred umbrella.

I choose to forget the image that made Charon weep –
East of the river Ota when he suckled at the banks,
he saw a manger of skulls weeping crayfish.

Antony Owen

SOUND BITES

I lied. This isn't me, this smile,
but, hey, please feel free to doubt it.

I know. I can't help it. Disarming.
It's a gift. This flashing smile,
perfect teeth, chiselled nose, twinkling eyes –
you can believe in them, can't you?
The full effect? Believe I me.
My svelte, lightly-tanned openness,
boy-next-door charm, up-and-coming
success-story striped tie, understated
elegance: you trust them, don't you?

Of course you do. I do myself
in daylight. Here. With the cameras.
In front of the Government buildings.

'Hi! Nice to see you! How's it going?'

I lied. Look, this is the truth now.
But my laugh says, 'Nonsense, he's joking!'
Quietly self-deprecating, that's all –
all the more likeable for it:
you trust me, don't you, little fish?

Don't say I didn't warn you, but
that's me there – above, behind my eyes,
hadn't you noticed? Yes, that's me
with the bright tiger-shark snout, cold
predatory jaws grinning upward
while you warm to my disguise…

Come a little closer, my friend,
come and chat to Tony.

Harry Owen

SCARLET MACAWS

The scarlet macaws want their red back,
not puce but rich rubescence.
They squawk and growl
for the people to give it back.

They want their green and yellow, the ultramarine
and azure of flight feathers.
They want their green homes to vibrate
against their red plumage.

They don't want to be eaten.
They don't want to be sacrificed.
They don't want to be shot for their celestial light
        and lose their eyes.
They don't want to be called Seven Macaw
        and mark the coming of the dry season
        or the hurricane season.

They don't want to be shot from the world tree
        by the Hero Twins
or be worn by them in a victory headdress.
They don't want to be bred as pets or for trade.

They want to spread their feathers
like the world's riches, a currency
that doesn't cost a thing, that doesn't
        symbolise blood.
They don't want their heads chopped off
        and stuck on poles in city temples.

They say their scarlet hue is life.
They say that every tree is an axis mundi
and all their eyes are suns.
They don't want their heads stuck on human bodies
     for funeral rites.

They don't want their ashes to treat diseases
because no medicine is left, no doctor.

They want to take their place
with the quetzal and the jaguar.
Their feathers are axes,
their feathers are lightning,
their feathers are rain

for everyone, not just the rulers with their royal aviaries.
Sun-macaws are free,
they are prayer-arrows,
Morning Stars,
they are the west wind that brings change.
They are the cardinal directions of health.

Do not bury them in human graves.
Do not bury them as plucked grave-goods
until the country is just a naked carcass
with its wings bound tight around its heart.

Pascale Petit

THE SPIDERS

a New Labour fallacy

The government here is largely
made up of spiders. They don't like us.

They tell us how lucky we are
to be ruled over by spiders

and how our enemies
are envious.

Only spiders
are rewarded with high positions

so we all want to be spiders
if it means getting on.

We don't like spiders
but we're resigned to becoming spiders

if that's what it takes to defeat
the spiders.

Ian Pindar

STABBERJOCKY

with apologies to Lewis Carroll

'Twas Brexit, and the slithy Gove
did frottercrutch in dwarfish glee;
he snicker-snacked the Camerove,
Machiavelliadastardly.

Beware the stabberjock, my son!
The empty eyes, the robo-glint!
who fellobrates the Murdocrone
the Ruperturtle übergimp!

He pallerised the BoJo cloon
they chummed upon their sunderbus
emblazoned it with fibberoons
and bambulluntruthoozled us.

The tousled toddler slaughterchopped,
his destiplans an Eton mess,
the slubbergubby gollumgove
a shadowhand of viciousness.

O gipperchund! And vomberblast!
The skitterchit of slick and sly
the snicker-snack of backstablades
the scrabblage to ruthlerise.

The bubberchut of charismissed
the turdletruck of banalbore
is patterfrondled on the head
a pawn upon a checkerboard.

Beware the stabberjock, my son!
The empty eyes, the robo-glint!
who fellobrates the Murdocrone
the Ruperturtle übergimp.

Steve Pottinger

SKY NEWS FROM THE GARDEN OF EDEN

Soldiers invade a hotel lounge fingering death.
A girl sits with her family – innocents.

Her dress is thin as this paper, her terror as white.
She holds up her hands like wheat to the scythe.

This gesture says: *We are nothing, spare us.*
We will live unseen beneath the body of a tank,
claim no sunlight, drink rain, eat insects.

Not even her eyes have fire enough
to touch these terrible gods.

Within the year her dress will be rags, she will grow old,
while others gather silk around their bellies, deal in oil.

Perhaps she's already dead, owning no grief, no grave,
no mark but this frail surrender on my screen.
I switch off. My tears leave nothing but salt.

                                        Gerard Rochford

Iraq is, by tradition, the site of the Garden of Eden.

THE DATE

Because Josef was Palestinian
we were turned away at the door
of the discotheque. He shrugged
and led me purposefully
to the car park beside the Dead Sea
where I taught him to drive,

weaving between sand dunes
in the headlights, until finally
we missed, rocking on a knoll
like a weighbeam, equally balanced
in some middle way, going nowhere.
Him an Arab, me a Jew, each wondering

how to move forward
into the darkness without letting go
of the steering wheel. A little in love
with revving the engine
into an oscillating fury of frustration
whilst plotting our escape together

in tense anxious voices.
Preferring this complication,
to the straight white road
back to Jerusalem.

                                                    Sue Shaw

RUBBISH

We pull our little rubbish houses
round us for comfort
and squinch down

we're frightened
don't take our house away
don't swipe the foodbank food from our plates
great hands of the mighty
are greedy hands

we pull our little houses snuggle-close
their thin walls won't bear the wolfish breath
huffing our house down

we're scared
great hands fling us to the wolf
not even the straws belong to us

Penelope Shuttle

CORBYN HAIKU

Jeremy is not
a typical leader – one
reason we love him

Hylda Sims

AVAILABLE LIGHT

Those trees now.
Just listen to them.
All the long night they've been rushed by
opinionated westerlies
imposing their shouting.

So I went to join
the tide's attempted
escape, but an empty beach
gave itself up to seething dark water
and then drowned there before

my ears. Transmitters.
It's the same old sound,
as ancient as the oceans,
the exhausting savaging white noise
of a storm rising ten,

its breakers broken
torn up from the sea.
Not easy to find the still life
in what's left of available light
to witness a quiet voice.

An uncut page though
waiting there inside
an old shelved book he gave me just
before my father died, glows vivid
equity, while listen,

there's leaking rain
trying to pulp it.
We preserve who we are as best
we can, but gales seize and dissolve us,
they soak up our silence.

Sean Street

POEM FOR JEREMY CORBYN

a parable of the signpost and the weathercock

The weathercock is varnished gilt,
revolves in every wind.
The signpost marks the road that mounts,
the miles you left behind.

You've walked so far, your breath is short,
with jaded eyes you scan
a wilderness of spin and spite
to find an honest man.

A paper storm infests your street,
the words return to air.
You pause, undress some walking suit
and find there's nothing there.

Without a wind, the puppets sag,
the paper turns to dust.
Yet still, you'll walk a thousand miles
to find a man you trust.

Merryn Williams

THROUGH

Glass, except when insects hit it,
dogs snort aggravation at it,
the rain runs down in tears,
has no particular problem with light.

'Go through,' says glass, 'I have no quarrel
with you', and light whangs on,
with no pause for refraction,
prepared to bounce or be absorbed.

Even when of colour; red of copper,
pink of manganese, frequencies get through
to shine their theatre lights on naves,
to place their spots, as ordered by the sun.

Only mirror-silver says 'You can't come by.
The in is separated from the out by you'.
All that lets in more than glass is air,
when at last you throw the windows wide.

Simon Williams

STROYKA 501

This is the place, says Lyudmila. *Start digging.*
They hit something metallic and begin scraping.

Rusty nails, a piece of track on the outskirts
of Salekhard, the capital of the Yamal Nenets

Autonomous Region. Once, a 10,000 year old
baby woolly mammoth was discovered buried

near here. It's in a museum now. An attraction.
But this is different. Construction Project 501.

The Great Plan for the Transformation of Nature.
A trans-Polar line stretching from Inta to Igarka,

its workforce, enemies of the people – poets,
a 16 year old orphan caught stealing beetroots

to feed her sisters, soldiers who'd been released
from prisoner-of-war camps, a fresh-faced

book-keeper whose employer's money was eaten
by rats that got in the safe. 300,000 not forgotten,

but not talked about either. A third of them dead
from execution, exhaustion or hunger. The cold

would have taken many more. 50 below in winter.
The project stopped when Stalin died. The tundra

took their bones with the tracks, kept the secret
for half a century. Lyudmila and others collect

statements, photos and letters for the archives,
for the descendants of prisoners and guards who live

side by side now, for future generations, for tourists
who arrive by helicopter. Rumour has it the quest

for gas will resurrect the Great Plan. Outside the gate
of Camp 48, a tourist unzips his padded jacket,

drinks vodka, then tips the remainder in the snow.
He leaves a potato and a loaf of bread before he goes.

Pat Winslow

SOMEONE HAPPENED

they like to pretend
it's all about him
but it's not
it's all about us

it's about our seeing
a glimmer of light
and crawling out from
underneath our misery,

about our being weary
of scratching a bare living
and being fed lies
for our supper

about our having tired
of huddling together
with the dreams we saw
unpicked at the seams

it's about our caring
I mean really caring
and feeling empowered
to change things

it's about throwing open
our windows and doors
to make way for sunshine
and clean air

and sneering they
say it's a joke or a cult
but really it's all
about hope

Someone crept in
and lit a candle in our hearts
that someone happened
to be him.

Abigail E.O. Wyatt

COMMON CAUSE

James Larkin was a man who would put a flower in a vase on a table as well as a loaf on a plate
– Sean O'Casey

First you need bread
then you need
a chair, or chairs,
and a rough-hewn table
on which to rest a vase

(crisp white linen would be a bonus, if available).

Then you need flowers,
not decorative
or anything so superfluous

but for good cheer,
to greet your reddened eyes
as you rattle open the door,
to remind you when you sit
of why the bread tastes good
and there should always be an extra slice.

Take this small sheaf of poems too
as you might the vase of roses
for they are meant to make common cause
with those who'd put a loaf on the plate –
now as much as ever before –
and to be read when bellies are growling or full.

Neil Young

THE POETS

Michael Bartholomew-Biggs is a former Reader in Computational Mathematics at the University of Hertfordshire. He now edits the online magazine *London Grip*.

Neil Beardmore is based in Milton Keynes. He won the Richard Burton Poetry Prize and his novel set in Goa, *Lemon Seas*, will be published later in 2016.

Ian Birchall is a historian, translator and author of several articles and books, particularly relating to the French Left. His website is laughingly called *Grim and Dim*.

Janine Booth describes herself as a 'performing angry middle-aged woman poet'. She is co-chair of the TUC Disabled Workers' Committee and has published *Autism and Equality in the Workplace*.

Alan Brownjohn, born 1931, has been a teacher and a Labour candidate and is now among the most eminent British poets. 'If people in the future want to know what many lives were like in the second half of the 20th century they should read Alan Brownjohn – observant, troubled, humane, scrupulous, wry, funny' (Anthony Thwaite). His poem has appeared in *The Saner Places* (2011).

Rip Bulkeley won the Society for Nautical Research's Anderson Medal for his scholarly work *Bellingshausen and the Russian Antarctic Expedition 1819-21*.

Olivia Byard's *The Wilding Eye: New and Selected Poems* was a *New Statesman* recommended read. Her poem was originally published in *Quadrant*.

Di Coffey is a one-time student nurse, ex freelance journalist, retired designer/maker of nursery mobiles, ex smallholding farmer, current vice-chair of Falmouth Labour Party. She cared for the love of her life, Dermot, for 17 years, and her debut pamphlet, *The Tugboatman's Daughter*, is sold in aid of the Multiple Sclerosis Society.

Deborah Cox is a member of Back Room Poets, Oxford, and was shortlisted for the Bridport Prize in 2008. She is currently putting together a collection, *Down and Out*, articulating hitherto subjected voices.

Barbara Cumbers worked for the Open University until retirement last year. Her poetry collection, *A Gap in the Rain*, is published by Indigo Dreams.

Simon Curtis (1943–2013) was a lecturer at Manchester University and edited the *Thomas Hardy Journal* for many years. He is very much missed.

Tony Curtis is one of the premier poets of Wales and a winner of the National Poetry Prize.

Ann Drysdale brought up three children as a single parent and now lives in a mining town in Gwent. Her latest poetry collection is *Miss Jekyll's Gardening Boots* (Shoestring Press). 'The Bigger Picture' was first published in *Quaintness and other Offences*.

Matthew Duggan was born in Bristol in 1971. His prizewinning collection *Dystopia 38.10* (erbacce press) will be published later in 2016.

John Freeman is a former lecturer at Cardiff University. He lives in Cowbridge.

Neil Fulwood lives in Nottingham and is a member of the Alan Sillitoe Committee.

Katherine Gallagher is an Australian living in England. Her poem is taken from *Passengers to the City* (Hale and Iremonger 1985).

Owen Gallagher lives in London where he worked as a primary school teacher. His latest poetry collection is *A Good Enough Love* (Salmon).

John Gohorry is a former lecturer in Further and Higher Education in North Hertfordshire. He has won many awards including the Keats-Shelley Poetry Prize.

Adrian Green is a Southend poet whose poems and reviews have appeared in magazines and anthologies at home and abroad. His latest collection is *Chorus and Coda* (Littoral Press).

Nicki Griffin lives in Ireland and is co-editor of the poetry newspaper *Skylight 47*.

Steve Griffiths's seventh collection is *Late Love Poems* (Cinnamon 2016). As a specialist in social and health policy, he has worked for charities and local and national government.

Paul Groves lives in Monmouth. He is a winner of multitudinous competitions, including the *Times Literary Supplement* International Poetry Prize (twice). His most recent collection is *Qwerty* (Seren).

Mark Haworth-Booth lives in Barnstaple. Now retired, he was a curator at the Victoria and Albert Museum.

Stuart Henson is a poet and playwright. *The Odin Stone* is available from Shoestring Press.

Kevin Higgins lives in Galway, Ireland. His fourth collection, *The Ghost in the Lobby*, was published by Salmon last year.

Norton Hodges's poem is loosely based on Shakespeare's ninety-fourth sonnet. He taught modern languages for 22 years and has also worked as a pay clerk, book reviewer, adult literacy tutor and examination invigilator. In 2005 he was awarded the Grand Prix International Solenzara.

Stephen Horsfall works at the HCN mail centre in Hemel Hempstead. He is a member of Open University Poets.

Mike Jenkins lives in Merthyr Tydfil. He is editor of *Red Poets Magazine*.

Helen Kidd's collection *Blue Weather* won the Cork Manuscript Award in 2003. She was co-editor of the *Virago Book of Love Poetry*, has taught Creative Writing and English Studies for many years and has also collaborated on cross-arts projects in the UK and Finland.

Louise Larchbourne recently returned to the acting career she left for motherhood some time ago. She is on the editorial team of *The Fat Damsel*, and is the current organiser of 'Ekphrasis Poetry at the Museum', a series of readings in situ of work inspired by the Ashmolean Museum in Oxford.

John Lucas is Professor Emeritus at the Universities of Loughborough and Nottingham Trent and the author of many literary and critical works. He now runs Shoestring Press. 'Blame' originally appeared in his 2007 collection *Flute Music*.

Thomas McColl works at the Vote Office in the Houses of Parliament which issues *Hansard* and other official documents. He tries to keep work and creative writing apart.

Alwyn Marriage is managing editor of Oversteps Books and holds a research fellowship at the University of Surrey. She has been part of a delegation of six British poets to Romania and her first novel is due out next spring.

Nicholas Murray is a Fellow of the Welsh Academy and has published several acclaimed biographies; *Matthew Arnold* (1997) was a *New York Times* Notable Book of the Year.

Antony Owen visited Hiroshima in 2015 to interview atomic bomb survivors. He is one of a handful of people appointed as CND (UK) Peace Education Patrons and his work generally explores the consequences of domestic and international conflicts.

Harry Owen emigrated from England to South Africa in 2008. He has published six collections of poetry and edited the anthologies *For Rhino in a Shrinking World* and *I Write Who I Am*, featuring the work of nineteen young poets from disadvantaged township schools in the Eastern Cape.

Pascale Petit has won many awards for her poetry and was chair of the judging panel for the 2015 T.S. Eliot Prize. Her seventh collection, *Mama Amazonica*, will be published by Bloodaxe Books in 2017. 'Scarlet Macaws' was previously published in *New Boots and Pantisocracies*.

Ian Pindar has published two poetry collections, *Emporium* and *Constellations* (Carcanet).

Steve Pottinger is a performance poet who has gigged all over the country. His book *more bees bigger bonnets* was chosen by the economist Richard Murphy as one of his books of the year in the *Times Higher Education Review* and his letter to Caffe Nero, taking them to task over their tax avoidance, went viral in 2014.

Gerard Rochford has published three collections: *Failing Light*, *Of Love and Water* and *Morning Crossword*. He appears in *Best 20 Scottish Poems, 2006*, chosen by Janice Galloway for the Scottish Poetry Library.

Sue Shaw is a writer of children's stories, formerly a journalist and teacher. She once found a seagull entangled in a fishing net and set it free.

Penelope Shuttle lives in Cornwall. Her new collection *Will you walk a little faster* will be published by Bloodaxe Books in 2017.

Hylda Sims's poetry is published by Hearing Eye. She runs a monthly poetry and music event, Fourth Friday, at the Poetry Café in Covent Garden.

Sean Street worked in radio for thirty years and was the first Professor of Radio at Bournemouth University.

Merryn Williams was the founding editor of *The Interpreter's House* and is literary adviser to the Wilfred Owen Association. Her fourth poetry collection, *Letter to my Rival*, is published by Shoestring Press.

Simon Williams is a journalist. He was elected the Bard of Exeter in 2013 and founded the large-format magazine *The Broadsheet*.

Pat Winslow is a Writer in Residence in a prison and a celebrant for the British Humanist Association. Her poem was a prizewinner in the Wilfred Owen Competition 2014.

Abigail Elizabeth Ottley Wyatt was born in the '50s into a working-class family; her father, Henry, was a plasterer, and his parents, Matilda and Percival, both worked in service in London. Acutely aware of her great good fortune in passing the 11+, she qualified as a teacher of English choosing to work within the comprehensive system. In 2004 she left the profession to concentrate on her own writing.

Neil Young hails from Belfast and now lives in north-east Scotland, where he is co-founder and one of the editors of *The Poets' Republic* magazine. *Lagan Voices* (Scryfa) is a Belfast memoir, and a pamphlet of fourteen sonnets, *The Parting Glass* (Tapsalteerie) was published in February.